811.54 H848Le
Howard, Ben.
Leaf, sunlight, asphalt

Y0-EIW-111

HISTORY & HUMANITIES

APR 2 2 2010

Other Books by Ben Howard

POETRY

Father of Waters: Poems 1965-1976
(Abattoir Editions: University of Nebraska at Omaha, 1979)

Northern Interior: Poems 1975-1982
(The Cummington Press, 1986)

Lenten Anniversaries: Poems 1982-1989
(The Cummington Press, 1990)

Midcentury
(Salmon Publishing, 1997)

Dark Pool
(Salmon Poetry, 2004)

PROSE

The Pressed Melodeon: Essays on Modern Irish Writing
(Story Line Press, 1996)

Leaf, Sunlight, Asphalt

BEN HOWARD

salmonpoetry

Published in 2009 by
Salmon Poetry
Cliffs of Moher, County Clare, Ireland
Website: www.salmonpoetry.com
Email: info@salmonpoetry.com

Copyright © Ben Howard 2009

ISBN 978-1-907056-13-0

All rights reserved. No part of this publication may be reproduced or transmitted in any form or by any means, electronic or mechanical, including photography, recording, or any information storage or retrieval system, without permission in writing from the publisher. The book is sold subject to the condition that it shall not, by way of trade or otherwise, be lent, resold or otherwise circulated without the publisher's prior consent in any form of binding or cover other than that in which it is published and without a similar condition, including this condition, being imposed on the subsequent purchaser.

Cover artwork: *Wicker Chair* by Hope Zaccagni
Cover design & typesetting: Siobhán Hutson
Printed in England by imprint*digital*.net

For Robin

Acknowledgements

Acknowledgements are due to the following publications in which some of these poems were previously published:

Agenda, *Cithara*, *Dharma Connection*, *The Formalist*, *New Hibernia Review*, *On Earth: The Journal of the National Resources Defense Council*, *The Recorder*, *Sewanee Review*, *Shenandoah*, and *Unsplendid*.

"Not Yet" was printed as a broadside by Jerry Reddan at the Tangram Press (Berkeley, California).

"Leaving Tralee" appeared in *180 More: Extraordinary Poems for Every Day*, ed. Billy Collins (Random House, 2005).

November morning.
On tile roofs, traces of snow.
Why should elation
Arise amidst such coldness?
Whose hands are these? Whose fingers?

Contents

I

The Glad Creators	13
Dublin in July	19
Beyond My Ken	22
An Afternoon at the Crown	23
A Wish for My Sixties	24
Open Mic	25
We Must Labor to be Beautiful	26
Leaving Tralee	27
Celebrant	28

II

Original Face	31
In Utero: June 1944	33
Prune Kringle	34
A Benediction	35
The Little Drummer Boy Considers a Sabbatical	36
33 RPM	37

III

Leaf, Sunlight, Asphalt	41
Western New York, 2008	42
Irondequoit, Oswego, Canisteo	43
Sanction	44
A Bow	45
Giving and Taking	46
Sandalwood	47
Still Life	48
One Time, One Meeting	49

"How Do You Get to Carnegie Hall?"	50
MU	51
Firewood and Ashes	52
A Glass of Wine	53
Shizen Ichimi	54
Elegy	55
At Notre Dame	56
The Empty Mirror	57
What I May Rely On	58

IV

Expecting Nothing	61
Right Livelihood	64
Not Yet	68
Notes	69

I

The Glad Creators

Watching the light die along the canal,
Recalling the glad creators, all
Who'd played a part in the miracle...
    — Brendan Kennelly, "Light Dying"

i.m. May O'Flaherty

I

Had I been born a decade earlier
I might have found myself in Dublin City,
An able novice gamely setting out,
Equipped with confidence and cautious diction
But all the same a lamb among those lions
Who frequented McDaid's and Davy Byrne's,
Reciting Yeats or Ferriter by heart
Or bellowing invectives to the rafters
Or sitting meekly with a ball of malt.
I might have hung my hat with Kavanagh's
Or backed a horse that no one else believed in—
The counterpart, if I may say it plainly,
Of all those cherished scripts and precious verses
That never saw the light, or if they did,
Were not to be regarded or remembered.
I might have strolled along the Grand Canal
Or greeted Behan on an evening walk
Up Baggot Street, or stopped at Parsons Bookshop
To turn the pages of O'Connor's latest
Or, if lucky, met the man himself,
Smartly dressed and ripe for conversation.
What better place for scintillating talk
Than Baggot Street, its sun-reflecting fanlights
Looking down on realists and dreamers?
What better place than Dublin, all its glory

Tarnished just enough to make it human
And all its grace reduced but not abandoned.

II

"What is this?" asks the Zen contemplative,
Divining that the undistinguished street
He's seen a thousand times is not banal
But like Traherne's an oriental marvel.
"What *was* that? I might ask of Dublin City,
Where words were not imperial adornments
Nor yet the currency of politicians
But were, it seems, the very nutriments
On which a culture aching for release
Fed its heart and fortified its mind.
"May your son become a bishop," Behan said
To the kind nun attending at his deathbed.
Outrageous, yes, but in its way humane.
What finer way to offer gratitude
Or fend off fear, than by the spoken word,
Flavored to be sure by irony
But none the worse for that. And afterward,
The solemn pageantry of hearse and drum,
Wherein the State that had imprisoned him
And banned his books saluted his cortege.
And all for doing nothing much of note
But writing well and speaking from the heart.

III

Rudest of men, Kavanagh compared
A foolish woman's animated mouth
To a skipping rope suspended from her ears,
As though conspicuous loquacity
Were neither to be savored nor admired
But treated as a breach of civic order.

Were that the case, Kavanagh himself
Might well have landed in a lightless cell
And spent his years conversing with the walls
Or venting his opinions to the vermin
Until, at last, descending into silence.
As it was, he spent his unencumbered,
Spacious hours in the Palace Bar
Conversing with the likes of Myles and Cronin,
As if to talk were not an irksome chore
But were, in truth, the stuff of life itself
And all the freight of adjective and adverb
Were not mere ornament or armament
But were the glowing essence of the world
Embodied in the freely spoken word.
How fitting that the bard of Baggot Street,
So long on notions and so short on tact,
Should find his truest locus in the sonnet,
That prison-cell of nuns and plaintive lovers,
And there compose his late insouciant songs
With only water to restore his soul
And only syllables for company.

IV

Flann O'Brien. Myles na gCopaleen.
A quiet man who rarely said a word,
He stored the richest treasures of his mind
Behind the masks of multiple personae.
Better to be silent than to cast
The one pearl before a crowd of mockers.
Better to retain it for the page,
Where, if all conditions were propitious,
Its lustre might endure. Who else but Myles
Would think to conjure out of Irish air
A ready cadre of ventriloquists
To escort dullards to the theatre,

Providing, thus, engaging repartee
For those less able than themselves? In time,
That cunning band, impatient with their pay,
Would stoop to threatening their witless charges.
"Deposit, sir, a fiver in my pocket
Or I will take the liberty of making
Salacious comments to your brother's wife."
Faced with such extortion, Dublin's dullest
Fell to writing notes to one another,
Lest some coarse inflammatory insult
Or subtle barb be channeled through their mouths.
In this, if in no other ways, they shared
The modus of their reticent creator,
Who played, at once, ventriloquist and dummy,
Maintaining silence when it served his need
Or speaking through his many-colored masks
Or giving voice to voices not his own.

V

Scourge of puritans and pietists,
He saw the self-invented Irish nation
As nothing nobler than a load of hay
Beneath whose weight the likes of Myles and Behan
Breathed as best they could. And yet he stayed,
His name no longer *Whelan* but *O'Faolain*,
And fashioned from his nation's wounded psyche,
As from its failing dreams, his master story.
O'Connell's flaws and De Valera's failures
And all the contradictions he recorded
Were, it seemed, refractions of his own.
A writer should be cold, he told O'Connor,
And ever-distant from his characters.
Yet what, if any, distance lay between
The seasoned author and his character,
A rough-hewn Mayo priest who found himself

Prevailed upon to bury an apostate?
The rogue had sent away his wife and children,
And lived for half a decade with his mistress,
Who now would have him buried as a Christian.
"I'll put a stop to that!" the priest declared,
But in the end, he nodded and consented,
Doing, we are told, "the human thing."
Could that not be a motto for O'Faolain,
Who was himself no stranger to temptation?
And what, in truth, inclined him toward the lady
Whose culture was as alien as England's
And whom he thought not beautiful but *stately*?
What but her words, as when she wrote of Dublin,
The most implacable buildings were lanced with light,
Or saw on Herbert Place a *sun-charged gauze.*
But was it words or what they signified
That caused a realist to choose romance
And wakened fancies in a skeptic's heart?

VI

Imagine, if you will, the well-stocked shelves
Of Parsons Bookshop and the well-worn stool
Where Kavanagh, who rarely cracked a book,
Studied racing forms or read his paper
Or flirted with the girl behind the counter.
Imagine him in tweeds, avoiding Behan,
Or turning to exchange a salutation
With Clarke or Montague or Mervyn Wall.
And if you're of a mind to offer blessings,
Then fashion one for May O'Flaherty
Who made a temple of a common shop,
A place of worship where the greenest poet
And hoariest of novelists could meet
And there pay tribute to that World of Letters
Which now we must envision through the lens

Of non-reflective glass, as if those pages
Typed on Remingtons and Olivettis
Were not the spirit's living monuments
But merely relics of another time.
And as for Miss O'Flaherty,
Imagine her discussing acquisitions
With Mary King, or freshening her window.
Or see her, now, in Owen Walsh's portrait,
A gray-haired, sensible, upstanding woman,
For whom the miracle of Parsons Bookshop
Was not the issue of a grand design
Nor yet the fruit of visionary thought.
"It was all an accident," she later said.
Had I been born a decade earlier,
I might have written sonnets in her honor
Or failing that, sung praises to her name.

Dublin in July

*When the self advances toward the ten thousand things,
that is called delusion;
When the ten thousand things advance toward the self,
that is called enlightenment.*

— Eihei Dogen, *Genjokoan*

I

The Four Courts bear the heat of late July
And down Dame Street the buses wheeze and belch
Their foul exhalations, wearing ads
For *Women on the Verge of HRT*
And images of lissome men and women
Vacationing in Portugal and Spain.
Whatever I was thinking when that siren
Erupted from the din, its two notes blaring,
Was gone before I knew it, leaving only
A quick impression of a speeding engine,
A red-faced driver screaming out his window,
The heads and shoulders of pedestrians
Turning to watch the swiftly passing show.
Where is the stillness at the heart of things?
Where the silence? Here in the midst of movement,
My own unquiet mind pursuing Dogen's
Notion that the hungry, angry self
Advancing toward the world creates delusion,
I listen for that stillness and that silence,
As though they might be heard in horns and sirens.

II

Take a walk down South Great George's Street,
Where seedy bars and not-so-great hotels
Consort with trendy restaurants and shops
And India commingles with Japan.
Here is a laundry, there an Oxfam outlet.
And everywhere the crowds, the jostling shoulders,
The cell phone bleating from a stylish belt.
Tonight we'll dine at Yamamori Noodles,
Tomorrow eat panini at the Bailey
Or Chicken Tikki at the Shalimar.
What has become of that revered, imagined
Dublin of O'Brien and O'Faolain,
Its taste as Irish as a ball of malt?
Look for it in Liverpool or Boston
Or conjure it yourself from pints of Guinness.
But here beware of Vespas when you cross
This street that's no more Irish than its name,
Where traffic comes in rolling, tidal swells
But now and then grows still, as if recalling
The ochre ethos of a slower time.

III

On Grafton Street the blonde contortionist
Taunts a man who leers, or seems to leer:
"We know what you're doing. Take your hand
Out of your pocket!" Flashing a practiced grin,
She bends her undulate, half-naked torso
Until her eyes are looking up her backside,
Her grin intact, her frame a human hairpin.
All that by way of warming up her body
And warming, too, the watchers who surround her
In attitudes of wonder and desire.
And now the main event, the fitting climax.
For no more money than would fill a hat,

She steps into a small, transparent cube
And rolls her supple limbs into a ball.
As though she were a relic under glass,
A sacred text preserved for contemplation,
She waits in stillness for the crowd's applause.
Call it if you must a holy show,
A spectacle unworthy of regard.
But did she not arrest the human tide
That now goes out, not waiting for her bow?

IV

The self advances to its hiding place,
This table where unnumbered pints of Guinness
Have left their autographs in broken crescents.
Revenants of raconteurs and poets—
O'Brien, Behan, Cronin, Kavanagh—
Come back to haunt this visitor, whose thirst
Is not so much for witty conversation
As for a stillness strangely to be found
Amidst the clinks of glasses and the slow,
Sustained consumption of a ball of malt.
High windows lend an air of the cathedral
And shed a friendly though impartial light
On malice and benevolence alike,
As though the bygone boos and panegyrics,
The lurid gossip and the florid tales
Of reputations won and quickly lost,
Were so much dust, now settled in its corner,
However bright its colors at the time,
However real its presence in this room.

Beyond My Ken

The Samsara Bar and Café, Dublin, 2004

The lights are low, the table lantern-lit.
How restful to be sitting in this place,
its bamboo screens suggestive of repose,
its sparse calligraphy replete with meanings
well beyond my ken. How fortunate
to find myself enclosed by these environs,
whose name means suffering, the never-ending
cycle of birth and death, the end result
of ignorance, aversion, and desire.
The waitress takes my order, unaware
that earlier tonight, unheralded,
a slender book was eased into the world.
I hold it to the lantern, knowing it mine,
but knowing also that its ink and paper
are no more mine than that calligraphy,
those rich, exotic dishes on the menu.
How apt to celebrate that glad event,
so long awaited and so much desired,
in this the palace of impermanence,
its charms a warning that no book will last
for very long, and therefore should be relished,
as presently I'm relishing this plate
of steaming vegetables and fragrant rice
whose name I duly note but won't remember.

An Afternoon at the Crown

Even as the rain is letting up
I'm hearing voices from the bar downstairs

And wondering if happiness is quite the word
For what communicates itself in waves

Of laughter, tides of unrelenting talk,
A sudden swell of indistinct opinions

And who knows what amalgam of remarks
And exclamations, expletives and answers.

Having a go at sausages and champ,
I'm listening, as if to pipe and bodhran,

To rhythms and exuberant crescendos,
Not knowing if it's happiness I'm hearing

Or maybe just the rowdy voice of fear
And resignation, dread and anxious longing.

I glance through dirty windows at the street
Where walkers hurry by beneath umbrellas.

What are the vital signs of happiness
If not those loud and undulating voices

That rise from many quarters but resemble
A single jubilant choir? It's not for me

To say, though what I'm hearing is contagious
And has for all its undefined abandon

Bestirred a feeling that could pass for joy
Despite the rain, the bleak uncertain street.

Belfast, 2004

A Wish for My Sixties

for Michael Longley

I would have this setting down of words
Occur as naturally and, yes,
As fluently as sitting down
For conversation over fish and chips
And water in a paneled snug,
Our subjects—poetry, of course,
But also parenthood, Stravinsky—
No more important than the ease
Of two old poets having lunch,
Their words well-chosen, to be sure,
But also quick and unimpeded.

Open Mic

One by one they rise to read their poems,
the Open Mic a plywood podium
set before the rows of folding chairs.
A father's heart attack, a failed affair,
an ailing mother's loss of memory,
a daughter's grievances—each person's story
unfolds in verse more regular than graceful,
its meters loud, its rhymes predictable,
but all the same a vehicle for pain
that otherwise might never have been known
for what it was, or held in such esteem.
Constrained by rules, restricted to a minute,
each lyric yields a temporary light,
each spoken word a momentary flame.

We Must Labor to be Beautiful

*True ease in writing comes
From art, not chance.* So spake
The arch-apologist
For craft that even craftsmen
May fail to hear or notice

If what is written sings
As easily as Anna
Moffo in her heyday
Or Mozart in his *Ave*:
Song that's made of rests,

Quarter notes, fermatas,
Chromatics, decrescendos,
But seems as effortless
As blood in healthy veins
Or water over stone.

Ease of singing comes
From scales, arpeggios,
The hour spent perfecting
A single trill or slur
Or glorious cadenza.

Why then should labor be
Demoted, disregarded,
Consigned to steerage while
The dancers flirt and twirl,
The dandies stroll and swagger?

And why should I, on hearing
Yet another lilting
Connemara air,
Mistake its craft for passion,
Its art for artless longing?

Leaving Tralee

What better place to set down furtive thoughts
than here at the Imperial Hotel
on Denny Street at seven in the morning?
Not so much imperial as mellow
and darkened by Victorian décor,
this dining room is vacant but for us,
that harried-looking waiter and the one
he waits on, namely me. As for the page
I'm writing over tea too hot to swallow
I see it as a sieve, through which the pungent
odor of last night's fish, the kitchen clatter,
the muted talk of patrons in the lobby,
and all the sights I have or haven't noticed
are passing to their final destination.
But even as I mutter my lament
for all things unredeemed, unrecognized,
I'm thinking of the Sunday afternoon
I pulled a yellowed journal from the shelf
and found in it the features of a dream
of which I had no other recollection,
no tension in the limbs or in the heart.
If it survives, that story of a ride
through cobbled streets in someone else's car,
it's in those sentences, themselves imperiled.
Lift up your voices, cries the aging hymn.
Lift up your cameras, your pens and notebooks,
lest the images that flash and fade—
those taut inflections in a fleeting voice—
be no more lasting than a passing thought
and no less formless than a jotted dream.

Celebrant

For Michael Davitt (1950-2005)

On the tape you made for me you're reading "Crannlaoch,"
As though your voice had risen out of water.
Your solemn lines commemorate Ó Direain,
Likening his presence to a tree.

Michael, let these lines commend your passion
Not for verse alone but for its making,
Which will of course continue in your absence
But lost in you a celebrant and friend.

II

Marion and Beth Howard, circa 1930

Original Face

*What was your original face
before your parents were born?*
           — Zen koan

When you ask me to remember
my fundamental face,
my face before my parents
and ancestors were born,

I recall a photograph
of Marion and Beth,
who later would become
my father and my mother

but then were in their twenties,
courting or newly married
and gliding in a rowboat
on the Mississippi River.

Marion holds the oars
poised above the water.
Dashing in his cap,
he glances over his shoulder,

while Beth, a camera
cradled in her lap,
smiles, as if content
to be riding in a boat

with Marion, who leans
forward, about to make
another skillful stroke.
His shirt is loose and white,

her jacket square and dark.
Their indistinct reflections
ripple on the waters
of what appears to be

a quiet, easeful slough.
Beyond them, rows of trees
bend toward the right,
as if to counterbalance

their boat's gentle momentum.
What currents, even then,
were trafficking between them?
What thoughts of work or children?

Ahead of them lay hardship
and all the hoarded thought
of forty years together.
But here, as if misfortune

were but a passing phantom,
the two of them look ready
and eager for a future
that will, in time, include

the son who can't be seen
but nonetheless abides
somewhere in those waters,
those high Midwestern clouds.

In Utero: June, 1944

Little soul, what will become of you?
Extracted from your tender habitat,
You'll have no notion of a world at war.
Early on, you'll see the speckled footage
And hear the names *Korea, Eisenhower.*
But all the same, you'll ride your wobbling bike

On streets remote from craters and grenades
And scented with the musk of fallen leaves.
Pretending to be Superman, you'll save
Defenseless children, leap from orange crates,
And fly through skies still open and untainted
Before returning to your desk and crayons,

Your lessons in arithmetic and grammar.
Unmarked by anything more damaging
Than cuts and scrapes and bullies on the playground,
You'll hold your own against repeated warnings
Of mushroom clouds and cities blown to dust
And nightmares of your own small house exploding,

As though your present state, so warmly wrapped
In aminotic heat and amply nourished,
Were not a threatened temporary shelter
But were the paradigm by which you'll live
For years to come, however dark the news
Or virulent the phantoms on the screen.

Prune Kringle

Prune kringle, it was called.
My job: to bring it home
intact, its flaky crust

still warm, its dark interior
sweet, thick, delicious.
I was a boy of ten,

old enough to stand
in Allen's Tea Room, coins
in hand, to count my change,

and safely to transport
that soft, mysterious treat
swaddled in cellophane.

Old enough, as well,
to feel your gratitude,
your pride in my attainments,

but not yet old enough
to know what care or pains
you took in my behalf

or what your worries cost
in sleep or muffled tears.
I was a thankless child,

and yet my weekly errand,
dutiful but relished,
brought you peace and comfort.

Even now I see you
testing its sticky fruit,
its sweetness on the tongue.

A Benediction

The Lord lift up his countenance upon you:
Unsought, unheralded, that noble line,
Itself an undulant, uplifting rhythm,
Arose to meet this morning's meditation,
Its melody a lilting obbligato
Heard above the drip of melting snow.
How could I have guessed, much less divined,
That gold so deeply buried in a psyche
Would show its colors at the end of March
Or that the dirt it carried on its journey
From then to now would swiftly wash away,
Leaving the thing itself, a perfect ingot
Denuded of its doctrinal accretions
And gorgeous as it was when first it fell
Into a soil that held it undefiled.

The Little Drummer Boy
Considers A Sabbatical

Don't kid yourself. I know what you're thinking.
"Here he comes again. He and his drum."
I know it's all predictable—the tinsel
Draped like spiders' webs on drooping branches,
The costly cards and breakable displays,
The incandescent camels on the lawns,
And, as if to usher in the lot
Or keep it moving to a steady beat,
The unrelenting rhythm of my drum.
I know you'd like it if I took my drum
And did the thing that's better left unmentioned
Or failing that, packed up my drum and drumsticks
And beat a path to Spain or Yucatan.
Don't think I haven't fathomed your disdain.
"Give it a rest!" I've almost heard you say
And truth to tell, I've more than once considered
Taking a well-earned leave in some warm spot
Where I could drink tequila or champagne
And, if luck should favor me again,
Compose another sentimental song.
But those are dreams, unlikely to come true,
And for the nonce, whatever you may think,
I have a duty and a job to do.
Look at this way, folks: not everyone
Is quite as old or cynical as you,
And though I know that endless repetition
Has put a certain tarnish on my charm,
If there is still a single open soul
With what the Zen-folks call beginner's mind,
Be sure that I'll be there to bring delight
As once I did to you, when you were younger
And heard without dismissal or dislike
The light and gentle tapping of my drum.

33 RPM

Dylan. Cash. Sinatra. Belafonte.
What could have seemed more constant than those voices,
Each a timbre unlike any other?
Not the sentiments their songs expressed
Nor yet their pulsing rhythms held attention
So much as their unprecedented selves,
Embodied in a rasp or lyric tenor,
Rugged bass or spoken baritone.
Who could have known that voices so commanding
Would, in time, grow hoarse or whisper-thin
Or that the selves inhabiting those timbres
Would prove no more enduring than the sough
Of wind, the roll of thunder? Even now
To hear them as they were is to recall
An old solidity of thought and feeling,
As though those cadences preserved in vinyl
Were not mere transitory exhalations
But were as tangible as cooling glass,
The self's original, unchanging vessel.

III

Leaf, Sunlight, Asphalt

"our transient fictions of name and form"
      — Chris Arthur

Those leaves outside my window
    lift lightly in the wind.
        That newly planted cypress

takes on a deeper greenness.
    This summer heat will pass,
        but here in late July

sunlight warms the foxgloves;
    the asphalt, rinsed by rain,
        looks blacker than before.

How pleasing are those names—
    buddleia, artemisia—
        which in our innocence

we lend to changing things.
    Fictions, yes, and dreams,
        but wholly necessary.

And think how desolate
    this insubstantial world
        would be without its names:

cypress, rain, July,
    magnolia, rose, lobelia,
        leaf, sunlight, asphalt.

Western New York, 2008

Merton, were you living at this moment
You wouldn't fail to note how *lucid silence*,
As you once called it, silence void of language
But resonant with unperturbed awareness,
Is growing rarer even as we speak.
In silence, you believed, the hills and forests
Bespoke themselves, absent self or Hearer.
To that condition, which eluded you
Even in your solitary hours,
You made it your vocation to aspire,
Fighting all the while your ego's need
To speak, be recognized, be deemed important.
The hills and forests that you left behind
Are still resounding in their silences
But everywhere, the clamor you decried
Is swelling in a violent crescendo.
Would that you might rejoin us to implore
Our anxious minds to hearken to themselves
And by the eloquence of your example
Enable us to listen and be still.

Irondequoit, Oswego, Canisteo

Piling as they will in mid-October
on unmown grass and still-intact impatiens,

those leaves could be the emblems of the names
that land on hills or settle into valleys

and later take their places on the maps
or in the histories of towns and cities,

as though they were indigenous as oak
or solid as the boulders on a mountain.

Irondequoit. Oswego. Canisteo.
Even to say them is to feel their weight,

though it's composed of little more than air
and though its content, felt or accidental,

may be at best a homely imitation
of things that are themselves no more substantial

than speeches that endured beyond the moment
and once-green forms that crumble underfoot.

Sanction

Even if a day
    should pass without the shrill
        intrusions of the news,

and even should the sight
    of cardinals at the feeder
        come to seem momentous,

nonetheless the old
    anxieties of loss
        and gain, uncertain health,

and all their darker cohorts
    will agitate that pond
        sometimes called the mind

unless, as happened late
    this morning, quietude,
        descending like a slow

and silent exhalation,
    should sanction as they are
        those robins on the lawn,

that fallen tree, whose trunk
    whitens in the sun,
        that swiftly moving cloud.

A Bow

> *The here and everywhere, the now and always of the poetic moment.*
> — Seamus Heaney

Now without its leaves, that Red-Twig Dogwood
could satisfy an appetite for order,

so unencumbered are its upswept branches,
no two alike but rising from a single

curvature of earth and leaf-strewn snow,
which always was, if not in this one yard

then in that everywhere to which such words
as these are but an homage and a bow.

Giving and Taking

i.m. Carol Burdick (1928-2008)

This pond that was your hourly companion,
    proferring its geese in late September,
its white reflected light in early March,
    is offering, just now, an April thaw.
At the far edge, among the reeds and grassses,
    some frightened animal is seeking cover.
You would have watched it with binoculars.
    You would have known its features and its name.
And all the while, what you were taking in
    would in its way have taken you as well,
as though your gift to geese or ice or junco
    were nothing more or less than your attention,
your undivided gaze across the water.

Sandalwood

This incense burning in its wooden holder
is not unlike the incense that I set

beside your urn while Kelsey read the book
you made for her, the book of ABC's,

each with its rhyming verse, its witty glance
at daily life, its motherly advice.

Truth to tell, you were her mother's mother,
and as the smoke was wafting past the pages

which she was turning slowly, one by one,
she was her mother's daughter, carrying on

whatever hurts were buried in your rhymes,
whatever hoarded tales her mother held

but wouldn't for the world have told her daughter,
lest the torch be passed, the hurt continued.

Better to let them rise, those wisps of smoke,
lending on their way their sweet aromas.

Still Life

Those ripening bananas,
    those pears that even now
        are turning dark and juicy:

who first produced that lie
    and conjured out of air
        the notion of a lasting,

picturesque repose?
    Even on that canvas,
        whose apples, plums, and bowl

appear to be at rest,
    the facts are otherwise.
        So it is this morning,

the first blue light arising
    behind those leafy branches—
        and on the page these black

characters purporting
    to catch the shapes of things,
        the flux of morning light.

One Time, One Meeting

Picking up the phone to call my son,
I entertain the thought that every act,
No matter how familiar or banal,
Might be construed as unrepeatable
And all of life as ceremonial.
What could be less formal than the feel
Of yet another handset in the hand
Or, beneath my fingertips, the cool
Resistance to the punching-in of numbers?
And what could be more normal than *hello*,
Spoken by a voice I couldn't fail
To recognize, despite the poor connection,
The fading in and out across the miles?
And yet to entertain that counter-thought,
To see each action and its consequence
As marvelous and not to be repeated,
Suffices to enlarge this conversation
Beyond the casual or circumstantial,
The morning's headlines and the evening's news,
As though just now the truth of things had spoken.

"How Do You Get to Carnegie Hall?"

Who wouldn't fear the darkened concert hall,
The silence settling on expectant faces?
Clammy hands. A turmoil in the belly.
And all because the moment has arrived
When every minute spent on making fingers
Do what they should do, and every hour
Devoted to a notion of perfection
Have brought this cloud-shape sometimes called a self
To just this place, where dreadful things can happen.
Whose music will arise from practised hands?
And who's the one who calmly seats himself,
Adjusts his stand, positions his guitar?
It all depends, his body seems to say,
As though the contours of an allemande
Were not so permanent as they appear
But were the offspring of the changing air,
The progeny of temperature and moisture,
The creatures of the meal he ate this morning.
Better not to dwell on those conditions.
Better to begin, as if this one
Occasion were the only one that mattered,
And what is called a self were but a venue,
An article of faith, a clear volition.

MU

> *Mu*: (lit. "nothing, not, nothingness"). Often used synonymously with *emptiness*. In Zen the word *Mu* is used to point directly at reality and has no discursive content.
> — Dennis Genpo Merzel,
> *The Path of the Human Being*

Now as I recall that rumbling city,
Where bikers paying homage to their maker
Converged like thunderclouds in early June,
Revving up while waiting at the stoplights
And leaning with their women into turns
As though the sweetest joy were to be moving
While sitting still, unbound, un-helmeted,

I'm thinking also of those pillared signs
That kept their vigil in the city center.
MU, they read, in fearless capitals,
Referring to a place of higher learning,
But also bringing emptiness to mind,
The emptiness residing in the sight
Of aging, happy men and wheels in motion.

Milwaukee, 2002
MU: Marquette University

Firewood and Ashes

Merely to be told by Eihei Dogen
That firewood does not turn into ashes
Is not enough to still the anxious mind
That sees in firewood a blackened ember
And in a hand its spotted late successor.

Nor is it quite enough to hear from Dogen
That summer is no prelude for the fall
And winter not an earnest for the spring
If all he means is that the thing itself
And not its fate deserves our full attention.

All the same, I'm glad for that reminder
To watch the sparks fly up from sinking logs
And listen to the hissing of the wood,
As though that spectacle were all there were
And all that might be known of burning matter.

A Glass of Wine

Without awareness I prepared my meals,
Vacuumed rugs whenever they were dirty,
And drank whatever wine was put before me,
As though such actions might go on for ever
And I were not an ordinary being
But one immune to change and hidden peril.

Now to peel an onion is to see
Its yellow skin as beautiful or ugly
And even dirt and breadcrumbs disappearing
Into a canister invite attention,
As does this glass of Pinot Grigio
Glowing in the early-evening light.

Shizen Ichimi

How far away those robed,
Severe aficionados
Of unremitting change,

Their human pyramids
In rows, their darkened *zendo*,
Their distant, mournful gong.

What have they to do
With paeans to wine and roses
And cries of vain desire

Or with those celebrations
Of lips, breasts, eyes,
The falling negligee?

Everything, I think,
This cool September morning,
These yellow leaves intact

But on the verge of falling,
These zinnias still red
As lips but losing color

And in these lines a bow
To transitory joys
And unreturning lives.

Elegy

i.m. Robert Turner, 1913-2005

For years you brought your will
To bear on fluent clay,
Until it came to you

To *let the piece decide*:
To notice *the way things form*
And, at a certain point,

To get out of the way. Now,
Your enterprise completed,
You've stepped aside entirely,

Letting your energetic,
Quiet forms prevail,
Each shape your signature.

Bob, this August light
Is waning as I write,
Recalling indistinctly

Your unassuming spirit,
Which once had voice and body
And presently abides

In this the pot you gave me,
When most of what I'd known
Was burning into ashes.

So let this single vessel,
Whose russet, earthy hues
Remind me of Sedona,

Decide what it should say,
Its grace your truest nature,
Its strength your monument.

At Notre Dame

Someone has put a hamburger into the hand
Of the stone Jesus conversing with His disciples,
A half-eaten burger still in its paper wrapper,
As if to say that no one must neglect
To eat, even when telling parables
Or comforting His followers, who listen
In attitudes of reverence and ardor.

The Empty Mirror

Tell me, if you can, why mere desire
Vanishes when circumstances alter,
As though it were a portion left uneaten
And later fed to dogs or washed away.
The plate is clean again, the table empty.

Tell me why deceptions come and go
As quickly as the vapor on a mirror,
Revealing what was present all along.
How vacant, now, that unassuming glass
In which you see your features as they are.

What I May Rely On

Turning into nothing, all those days
Remain in memory, as though their patterns
Persisted when their dyes had long since faded.
Here is the morning sun. And here is dusk
Consuming every tree on the horizon.

Turning into forms of which I know
Only a little now, my own two hands
Tell me that the bones beneath that skin
Are what I may rely on to continue,
Whatever may become of mark or wrinkle.

IV

Expecting Nothing

Even before you were born,
your parents were expecting.
What have you done since then
but meet their expectations
or, as the case may be,
fall short? So now, if I
should ask you for a moment

to live without those framing
goals and stipulations,
those blinding expectations,
my modest proposition
might seem another mandate
which you, for good or ill,
must heed or disregard.

But let me, nonetheless,
invite you to envision
a day without the notions
of parents, priests, and teachers,
a day of rest and leisure
and dauntless exploration—
no lark or summer picnic

but a gate through which, for once,
you might conduct yourself,
seeing, as if you'd never
laid eyes on them before,
the street-sign at the corner
bent at a quirky angle,
the first forsythia

turning from brown to yellow,
the disappearing moon
at seven in the morning.

And should you feel impelled
by temperament or habit
to classify such sights
or assign defining names,

to praise, dispraise, or grade
that stranger's way of walking,
that Chrysler's peeling paint,
that odd, disheveled man,
let me suggest to you
that the clanking garbage truck
expelling noxious fumes,

those potholes left to deepen
for lack of funds or caring,
that elderly volunteer
delivering Meals on Wheels,
those tulips pushing up
through newly loosened soil,
are, at this one moment,

all there is. And as
you cross that dangerous street,
looking from left to right,
let me propose to you
that the venue you will enter,
prepared or unprepared,
in your envisioned future

will be no foreign field
nor alien terrain
but a self to which you've come
exactly as you are.
In time that formless form,
composed of mind and limb,
desire and circumstance,

may prosper and acquire
stature, rank, and power.
But may you also step
lightly into the light
of yet another morning
and into the stranger light
of dusk, expecting nothing.

For the Phi Beta Kappa Initiation Ceremony
Alfred University, April 7, 2004

Right Livelihood

On the occasion of my retirement

How shall I address you,
you to whom I gave
my youth, my middle age,
and much of my regard?
Now that I'm taking leave

of you, and you are backing
swiftly away from me,
how shall I name your features,
which even now recede,
as does the din of voices,

the clamor of demands?
What shall I call you now,
you who were not opaque
nor ever very solid,
your meetings, consultations,

syllabi, appointments
at most an aggregate
to which the name Professor
attached itself, as if
to give that ever-shifting

scaffolding of duties
and transitory desires
a look of permanence
and lasting aspiration?
Say, if you will, that all

those hours disappearing
even as I write,
those hours spent preparing
to say what might be said
of metaphor or meter,

O'Faolain's ironies
or Yeats's layered symbols,
do not reside in fraying
folders, yellowed notes
or boxes in a closet,

but are as living beings
inhabiting the wakened
minds of Claire and Jason,
Scott and Domenica,
and all those other seekers

who trusted me to listen
and, when apt, to guide
their nascent understandings
into a lit arena
or call to their attention

channels that otherwise
might never have been opened.
To them I dedicate
these lines, as well I might,
for in their widened hearts

and slow-maturing minds
is my continuation.
But what shall I say to *you*,
my erstwhile Superintendent,
who summoned me to quarrels

I'd rather have avoided
and when it suited you
subjected me to judgments
better left unspoken?
On more than one occasion

Larkin called you Toad,
a graceless epithet,
though not entirely false.
Frog, I might have said,
though not the frog that brought

enlightenment to Basho.
Rather, the one who croaks
in low, unmannerly tones
whenever he is hungry
or longing for his way.

I might have other names,
not all of them benign,
but today the crocuses
are up, and casting glances
backward or askance

is not my inclination.
So let me take a leaf
from Basho's heritage
and call you by a name
reserved for such employment

as does more good than harm,
a name appropriate
to rescuers and monks,
priests and clowns alike.
Right Livelihood, it's called,

and though your character
is not a priest's or hero's
much less a martyred saint's,
the livelihood you offered
was right enough for me,

providing as it did
a forum for reminding
the most recalcitrant
that every waking moment
is worthy of attention

and worthy, too, of words
chosen with precision
and truthful to the core.
Right speech, it's sometimes called,
by which is meant the speech

that indicates what's there
and never what is not;
that waters seeds of joy
and equanimity;
and, when warranted,

assigns revealing names
to greed and cruelty,
injustice and deceit.
So let me raise a cup
in gratitude to you,

Right Livelihood, who fostered
right and noble speech
in all of us who sought it,
as though it were your offspring,
your one enduring son.

April, 2006

Not Yet

Give me, if you will, a little time
To understand how meanings come and go,
Resembling ants converging at an anthill
And then dispersing, each with work to do.
Meanwhile, the anthill rises and expands.
The sun comes out. The days grow ever shorter.

Give me time to sense how meanings perish
Like plums left unattended in a bowl.
Because their lives were finite in the first place,
That spreading mold should come as no surprise.
So it is with meanings, I suppose,
Though how and why I've yet to understand.

Notes

The Glad Creators: For some of the details in this poem, I am indebted to Brendan Lynch's *Parsons Bookshop: At the Heart of Bohemian Dublin 1949-1989* (Liffey Press, 2006), Maurice Harmon's *Sean O'Faolain: A Life* (Constable, 1994), and *The Best of Myles: Flann O'Brien* (Dalkey Archive, 1999).

We Must Labor to Be Beautiful: The title of this poem is taken from Yeats's "Adam's Curse." The italicized quotation may be found in Alexander Pope's *Essay on Criticism*, ll. 362-63.

Leaf, Sunlight, Asphalt: See Chris Arthur's essay "Safety in Numbers," *Irish Pages* (Spring/Summer 2003), p. 73.

Elegy: The italicized phrases are taken from Robert Turner's reflections on his work. See *Robert Turner: Shaping Silence—A Life in Clay* by Marsha Miro and Tony Hepburn (Kodansha, 2003), p. 24.

One Time, One Meeting: The motto *ichigo ichie*, commonly translated as "one time, one meeting," has its origin in the Japanese tea ceremony. Each gathering in the tea hut is to be seen as unprecedented and unrepeatable. See *Zen Word, Zen Calligraphy*, by Eido Tai Shimano and Kōgetsu Tani (Shambhala, 1995), p. 35.

"How Do You Get to Carnegie Hall?" Once a stranger approached the violinist Jascha Heifetz on a street in New York City. "How do you get to Carnegie Hall?" the stranger asked. "Practice, practice, practice," Heifetz replied.

Shizen Ichimi: "poetry and Zen are one."

Praise for *Dark Pool* (Salmon, 2004)

Howard is another American poet captivated by Ireland to—one can't help thinking—the good of his craft. He writes just about the most natural, musical iambic line around these days, primarily in a propulsive, precise, and vocal blank verse but also in sonnets, quatrains, and unrhymed forms. It's as seductive of the inner ear as Irish storytelling is of the outer, gently drawing attention to large, subtle meanings.

—Ray Olson, *Booklist*

What gives these poems particular power is the honesty with which they explore the poet's lacks and absences, the gaps that he seeks to understand in his own life through these poetic explorations.

—Marc Conner, *Shenandoah*

Praise for *Midcentury* (Salmon, 1997)

Midcentury is a rewarding read, its iambic pentameter like the beating of a heart, its language by turns conversational and erudite and its resolution moving, if not exactly comforting. The narrator... emerges as a man of our own time, slightly at odds with the ways of the world but human and recognizably one of us.

—Patrick Chapman

Elegant, elegiac, casual yet moving, Ben Howard's poetry is both contemporary and classic. It spans eras and countries, fusing a fictional voice with a poet's own real obsessions. Ben Howard, besides being a fine poet, is a classical guitarist. The structure of Midcentury is like a great symphony, the kind that, moment to moment, is intimate, and yet its overall reach is almost beyond human grasp.

—Michael Stephens